Easy and Healthy
Japanese Food
for the
American Kitchen

Easy and Healthy
Japanese Food
for the
American Kitchen

Keiko · Ó · Aoki

Photographs by Susumu Miyamoto

Quill
Driver
Books

Sanger, California

Printed in the United States of America

Published by Quill Driver Books/Word Dancer Press, Inc.
1254 Commerce Way
Sanger, California 93657
559-876-2170 • 1-800-497-4909 • FAX 559-876-2180

QuillDriverBooks.com
Info@QuillDriverBooks.com

Quill Driver Books' titles may be purchased in quantity at special discounts for educational, fund-raising, training, business, or promotional use. Please contact Special Markets, Quill Driver Books/Word Dancer Press, Inc., at the above address, toll-free at 1-800-497-4909, or by e-mail: Info@QuillDriverBooks.com

Quill Driver Books/Word Dancer Press, Inc. project cadre:
Doris Hall, Linda Kay Hardie, Stephen Blake Mettee, Carlos Olivas, Andrea Wright

Quill Driver Books and colophon are trademarks of
Quill Driver Books/Word Dancer Press, Inc.
First printing

ISBN 1-884956-67-X • 978-1884956-67-6

To order another copy of this book, please call
1-800-497-4909

Library of Congress Cataloging-in-Publication Data

1. Aoki, Keiko O.
 Easy & healthy Japanese food for the American kitchen / by Keiko O Aoki.
  p. cm.
 Includes index.
ISBN 1-884956-67-X
1. Cookery, Japanese. 2. Quick and easy cookery.
I. Title. II. Title: Easy and healthy Japanese food for the American kitchen.
TX724.5.J3A74 2007
641.5952—dc22

2007001610

Table of Contents

Introduction

Most cookbooks are written by chefs, aimed at people who already know how to whip up a fancy meal and who are seeking new recipes to add to their repertoire. This book also has new recipes you've probably never seen in a cookbook, but that's where the similarity ends. I do not claim to be an expert chef, and my readers don't need to be experts either. My audience is the men and women who may not have the time to cook but who still want to prepare healthy meals for themselves and their families, meals that don't take a lot of preparation time and don't cost a fortune.

I was born in Tokyo but I now live in New York City where there are more restaurants on every block than probably anywhere else in the world. When I first came here, I never cooked. Either I ate out at one of these restaurants with friends, or went to some event where there was food served. I was too busy running a business and filling my social calendar to find the time to cook. What changed my attitude was meeting my husband, Rocky Aoki. Rocky is the founder of the Benihana restaurant chain. When I started dating Rocky, he was always running from one doctor's appointment to another.

In his youth, Rocky had been quite the daring young man, flying balloons over the Pacific ocean and racing speedboats, but some of his stunts ended badly and his accidents have taken a toll on his body. I decided that the best way to restore Rocky's health was to cook traditional Japanese meals for him. After all, if people in Japan live longer than in any other place on Earth, it seemed obvious that there was something in our food that promoted good health. And it worked. Today the only time Rocky goes to the doctor is to get an occasional checkup.

My busy New York lifestyle may have kept me out of the kitchen for many years, but I'd learned how to cook Japanese food from a real expert, my mother. When I was growing up in Tokyo, she taught me how to prepare our native dishes. But before she taught me how to cook, she taught me how to shop, which to a Japanese housewife is very important.

You see, Japanese food is healthy because all the ingredients must be fresh. A Japanese housewife shops every day. And not first thing in the morning. She waits until the afternoon. Why? Because Japan is such a small country, fresh food can be delivered from the farm or the sea to the market on the same day. So in the afternoon, the fresh food markets receive their daily supply of vegetables, fruits, meat, and fish. That's why if a Japanese mother wants to give her family the absolute freshest food, she knows to shop in the afternoon.

Because of this emphasis on freshness, Japanese cuisine changes with the seasons. In the spring, dishes that feature green-leaf vegetables like spinach will be served. In summer it might be rice with peas that were picked that morning. In the fall, when rice is harvested, the menu will feature this new rice with mushrooms. In winter you'll see only root vegetables, like turnips, as well as lots of crab meat and clams. This seasonality even extends to the table decorations. In spring your plate might be decorated with some cherry blossoms, while in the fall the table may have some fallen leaves.

To a Japanese, food must please the eye as well as the palate. A chef in Japan is considered to be an artist, and presentation is an important part of his job. Your guests will react to whatever you serve by what they see before they taste the food. You want to put them into the right frame of mind for your meal as soon as they sit down to the table by giving them the proper presentation. Japanese decorations are very simple; as I mentioned, a leaf or two might be all that is required, so the presentation will not add many minutes to the overall preparation time.

The presentation is even more important when introducing new food, particularly to children. Some children don't like the idea of trying unfamiliar foods. But, if instead of just serving Japanese food, you make it into more of an event, you'll have greater success. Just getting them to try using chopsticks can make it fun. If they get frustrated, then let them switch to a fork.

Of course Rocky's health didn't improve because of the presentation, but rather because of the ingredients in Japanese food. As I just told you, the ingredients overall tend to be very fresh, which means they retain all their nutrients. Also, in Japan we don't eat a lot of red meat but there's no doubt that the large quantities that Americans tend to devour is harmful. And we Japanese tend to eat smaller quantities altogether, and that not only keeps us leaner, but also healthier. Finally, there are ingredients that Japanese eat almost every day which promote good health which are mostly absent from the American diet, primarily soy beans which are used in various ways including miso and natto, both of which are basically fermented soybeans.

The Japanese people enjoy the highest longevity of any people in the world. That is not an accident. Some of the properties of fermented soybeans have been scientifically proven, such as their ability to reduce blood clots and prevent heart attacks. But we Japanese also believe, and there is some evidence for it, that products like miso and natto also prevent cancer, lower cholesterol, have an antibiotic effect, improve digestion, prevent obesity, and reduce the effects of aging. And, as a woman, I have no doubt that if the skin of Japanese women is so beautiful as many say, the underlying reason is their diet. So to me, Japanese cooking equals better health, longer life, and greater beauty. What more can you ask for?

And for older women, you should know that soy contains hormones that may alleviate the symptoms of menopause. Considering that taking artificial hormones, via hormone replacement therapy, has been shown to cause breast cancer, eating lots of soy might be an alternative for many older women.

Another food product used in Japanese cooking that is very healthful is rice vinegar. Vinegar is added to the rice used in sushi. We Japanese believe that vinegar promotes good digestion. That's why people who eat a lot of sushi don't feel bloated the next day. It's the vinegar in the sushi rice that helps one digest it.

I believed the Japanese cooking was healthful, and I proved that it worked with Rocky.

Some of the reasons many Americans don't cook Japanese meals is that they feel it is too difficult. They think special skills are required and they assume it is hard to get the proper ingredients. Actually cooking Japanese food is very easy, because the ingredients we use are simple, and we don't prepare complicated sauces like the ones used in Europe.

I too was worried that I couldn't get the ingredients I needed at my local supermarkets. But to my delight, I found that wasn't the case at all. First of all, some basic ingredients, like miso and soy sauce, are readily available in most supermarkets. When I was preparing each recipe, if I found it difficult to get a particular ingredient, I used an easier-to-find substitute which I have provided for you in the recipes. So for the most part, I guarantee you that you won't have a hard time finding the proper ingredients. There are a few ingredients that are a little harder to find, but I've listed where you can order these on the Internet, and once you stock up on them, you'll be all set.

And I also worked very hard to take away the final potential obstacle to cooking healthy Japanese food: time. I worked on these recipes so that in no case should they take more than thirty minutes or so, and many take even less than that.

In this book I provide you with recipes that will be easy to prepare, will be healthy for you and your family, and won't cost very much. All I can say now is, what are you waiting for, get cooking!

Special
Note

Many of these
recipes call for
making a sauce,
marinade, or
seasoning.
To simplify your
cooking, I suggest
you always make
this part of the
recipe first.

Basic Japanese Food Ingredients

Many ingredients for Japanese cuisine are readily available at better grocery stores. If you are having trouble finding some ingredients, try ordering them online. Two companies that have a good selection of Japanese food and utensils such as sushi mats are AsianFoodGrocer.com and PacificEastWest.com.

CURRY POWDER

Curry powder is a combination of spices. It was first made by the British who wanted to bring home the flavors of colonial Indian cooking back to Britain. Curry powder was brought to Japan at the end of the 19th century and quickly became very popular. While most curry powders include coriander, tumeric and cumin, each brand has a long list of various spices. Japanese curry has its own combination of spices, the contents of which continue to evolve.

SB International Corporation
www.sbfoods.co.jp
310-327-7000

DASHI

Dashi is the basis of many Japanese soups. It is most commonly made from dried fish (usually bonito) but it can also be made from dried kelp, or dried mushrooms. While it can be prepared at home, it's easier to just buy the prepared kind.

Ajinomoto USA Inc
www.ajiusafood.com
773-714-1436

MISO

Miso is a paste made from fermenting soybeans. It can also be made with rice or barley and, including regional varieties, there are dozens of types of miso sold in Japan, each with its own flavor and aroma. The soybeans are combined with salt and koji, a fungus used in the fermentation process. (Koji is also used when fermenting rice to make sake.)

Miso is protein rich and also contains many vitamins and minerals. It is a staple of Japanese cuisine. Miso soup is eaten by many Japanese for breakfast. Because cooking miso causes it to lose some of its nutritional value, it is usually added only after the soup or other ingredients have cooled a bit.

Marukome USA Inc
www.marukome.co.jp

HOT JAPANESE MUSTARD (WARAGARASHI)

This very pungent mustard is made from the seeds of the black rape plant and is used in many dressings.

SB International Corporation
www.sbfoods.co.jp
310-327-7000

NORI

Nori are sheets of edible seaweed used in Japanese cooking. It is best-known as the wrap for various rolls, like the California roll, found in sushi restaurants.

Yamamotoyama of America
www.yamamotoyama.com
909-594-7356

WASABI

Wasabi is a type of Japanese cabbage, the roots of which, when ground up, are very pungent, like horse radish. Once found growing along streams in Japan, most wasabi now is cultivated. Unlike peppers, the effect of which is felt on the palate, wasabi's strongest effect is on the nasal passages.

PANKO

Panko is the term used in Japan for bread crumbs. Panko is different than western bread crumbs as it has a crisper and airier texture. Made from wheat bread, it is used for coating fried food.

PONZU

Ponzu is a citrus-based sauce used in Japanese cooking.

Mizkan Americas, Inc
www.mizkan.com
847-590-0059

RICE VINEGAR (KOMEZU)

This vinegar is milder and has a gentler flavor than vinegars made from wine or fruit. Rice vinegars that are fermented for several months are superior in quality to those that are synthesized. Like all vinegars, rice vinegar helps to preserve food and keeps vegetables from discoloring.

Mizkan Americas, Inc
www.mizkan.com
847-590-0059

SAKE

Sake is an alcoholic beverage made from fermented rice. Japanese cuisine uses it as a flavoring agent the way wine is used in western cooking. Sake also helps to tenderize meat and counteracts strong flavors.

Takara Sake USA Inc
www.takarasake.com
510-540-8250

SOY SAUCE

Soy sauce is made from soybeans, wheat, and salt. Soy sauce is naturally brewed and used as a seasoning in cooking or as a table-top seasoning instead of salt. Because of the high sodium content of regular soy sauce, low-salt varieties are also now available for those who must limit their intake of salt.

Yamasa Corporation USA
www.yamasausa.com

TOFU

Similar to the way the people in the West make cheese from milk, Asian cultures make tofu from soy milk. Different Asian cultures use a variety of methods of coagulating the soy milk. The main coagulant used in Japan is *nigari*, which consists mostly of magnesium chloride that is extracted from sea water. Most tofu made in the U.S. is made with calcium chloride. There is no difference in the taste. Tofu is sold in several categories of texture, from soft (also called silken) to firm. Tofu is high in protein—especially firm tofu, over 10 percent of which is protein—while it is low in calories. Tofu contains no cholesterol and has nutrients such as iron, making it a healthy substitute for meat.

Morinaga Nutritional Foods Inc
www.morinu.com

Miso Soup

みそ
汁

Keiko's Miso Soup

(Serves 4)

Cooking Time: 10 minutes

Miso soup is an essential item in Japanese people's lifestyle. Consuming miso has many positive variables that we are unaware of. I drink miso soup every day in the morning with my husband. The Japanese believe miso has the effect of eliminating radioactive substances from the human body and the effect of rejuvenating damaged cells. Soybeans are rich in anti-oxidant such as vitamin E, but miso has a stronger anti-oxidation effect. As miso ages, the color becomes deep brown. The brown substance is called melanoidine that suppresses the production of fat peroxide in the body.

Ingredients:

tofu—firm	6 oz
spinach	5 bunches

Miso Soup Base:

dashi stock powder	1 Tbs
water	4 cups
miso	4 Tbs

Directions:

(1) First, we will make the soup base. In a pot, add water and bring to boil, mix in dashi stock powder and let it dissolve. Add the miso and let it dissolve.

(2) Cut the tofu in ¼-inch cubes and place in the stock and add it to the soup base, bring to boil.

(3) Add the finely chopped green spinach and serve in miso soup bowls.

Mom's Taste-Little Neck Clams and Spinach Miso Soup

(Serves 4)

Cooking Time: 15 minutes

The scent of miso soup brings memories of growing up in Japan. I'd love to share my beauty secret hidden behind miso soup. Linoleic acid contained in miso is known to stimulate the sebaceous gland to promote baby-like soft skin texture. This explains why many people say that Japanese women have very beautiful skin! Not only is the soup delicious but it provides wonderful benefits to your body.

Ingredients:

clams	16
spinach	5 medium-size bunches

Miso Soup Base:

dashi stock powder (dashi no moto)	1 Tbs
water	4 cups
miso	4 Tbs

Directions:

(1)　First, we will make the soup base. In a pot, add water and bring to boil, mix in dashi stock powder and let it dissolve. Turn the heat down to simmer.

(2)　Put the clams in a bowl and fill with cold water. Let sit until sand is removed from the clams. Under running water, wash and clean the clams' surface.

(3)　On a cutting board, cut the spinach into 3½ inch wide pieces. Set it aside.

(4)　Add the cleaned clams to the soup base. When all the clams have opened, add the miso paste and let it dissolve. Add the spinach at the end and, after just a few minutes, remove from heat. Serve in miso soup bowls.

Sushi & Rice

寿司
Sushi

&

ご飯
Rice

Bamboo rolling mats are essential for making sushi.
They may be obtained at any Asian food store or from online retailers.

Simply Delicious Gohan (Rice)

(Serves 4)

Cooking Time: 30 minutes

Being Japanese, Rocky, my husband, and I can't live without rice. Sometimes
when I go without having rice too long, my body automatically craves it.
Today, we can get delicious California-grown Japanese-style rice, so I suggest you use it.

Ingredients:

California rice washed and drained*	2½ cups
water	2½ cups

Directions:

(1)   Under running water, rinse the rice and drain. In a heavy pot, measure in an
amount of water equal to the amount of rice and let it sit for 30 minutes. This
is one of the important secrets in making delicious rice!

(2)   Cover and heat over medium flame. Just before it reaches the boiling point, turn the
heat up slightly and bring to a boil.

(3)   As soon as it boils, turn the heat to low. Simmer for 20 minutes until all the liquid is
absorbed. Turn the heat back up and cook for 10 seconds, remove from heat.

(4)   Let it stand for at least 20 minutes, keeping the lid on to absorb any excess moisture.

*Please make sure to use Japanese-style short grain rice only! No substitutions.

If you are making the rice with a rice cooker (highly recommended)
use your regular setting for white rice.

Keiko's Easy Fresh Tuna Over Rice

(Serves 4)

Cooking Time: 20 minutes

If you feel like making sushi at home, but don't feel like making the rolls, here is a simple way to satisfy your sushi craving!

Ingredients:

sashimi quality raw tuna	14 oz thinly sliced
basil	10 leaves
garlic	1 clove
green onion	1 medium sized
cooked California rice (white or brown)	4 servings

Marinade:

Tabasco sauce	to taste
salt, pepper	to taste
soy sauce	2 Tbs
vegetable oil	2 Tbs

Directions:

(1)   In a small bowl, mix all ingredients for the marinade and set aside.

(2)   On a plate, place the thinly sliced tuna. Pour the marinade over the tuna.

(3)   On a cutting board, thinly slice the garlic. Using your fingers, tear the basil leaves into small pieces. Sprinkle the basil over the tuna and marinade. Let sit for 10 minutes.

(4)   On a cutting board, chop the green onion into small pieces.

(5)   Divide and place the rice into 4 small bowls. Lay the tuna over the rice with the basil and garlic. To finish, garnish on top with the green onion.

Make the marinade first to simplify your cooking. If you are unable to find sashimi quality raw tuna, you can purchase a regular tuna and sear it to use as a replacement.

Yummy Ginger Rice

(Serves 4)

Cooking Time: 30 minutes

Ginger and chicken go hand in hand as their flavors complement each other well. This mixture makes a refreshing addition to rice, bringing out the classic home-cooking flavor of Japan.

Ingredients:

fresh ginger, peeled and thinly shredded	6 oz
California rice	4 cups
boneless chicken breast	7 oz
water	

Marinade for Chicken:

light soy sauce	4 Tbs
sake	4 Tbs

Seasoning for Rice:

light soy sauce	4 Tbs
sake	4 Tbs

Directions:

(1) In a small bowl, mix the ingredients for the marinade and set it aside.

(2) Under running water, wash the rice well and drain.

(3) Cut the chicken into small pieces. Place marinade in a shallow pan and add the chicken, turning to cover all sides.

(4) Take the peeled fresh ginger and cut into thinly shredded pieces.

(5) In a rice cooker, add the rice seasoning with the rice and the correct amount of water to cook the rice.

(6) Drip excess marinade from the chicken and add the chicken and the fresh ginger to the rice cooker.

If you don't have a rice cooker, follow the directions for Simply Delicious Gohan on page 10.

Keiko's Easy Sushi Rolls

Make the following sushi rice recipe for each sushi roll.
You will need to use a bamboo rolling mat to make the rolls.

Sushi Rice

(Serves 4)
Cooking Time: 30 minutes

One of my favorite activities is to invite some girlfriends to a sushi party. We get together at my place and make the rolls together. The fun part is eating the rolls we made with Japanese tea and accompanied by wonderful conversation.

Ingredients:

California short grain rice—cooked	4 cups

Seasoning:

rice vinegar	¾ cup
sugar	4 Tbs
salt	1½ Tbs
dashi stock powder	1 tsp

Directions:

(1) In a bowl, mix all seasoning ingredients and set aside.

(2) Place the cooked rice in a large mixing bowl. Sprinkle one third of the seasoning over the rice. Quickly and lightly cut and fold the rice on itself with a wooden rice paddle. Do not stir or beat the rice as this breaks the grains. Fan the rice to cool it during the time you are blending the rice with the cut and fold motion. Continue this process by adding the remaining seasoning little by little. Avoid making the rice too gooey.

(3) Cover the mixing bowl with a damp paper towel and set it aside for later use.

Spicy Tuna Sushi

(Serves 4)
Cooking Time: 20 minutes

Ingredients:

sushi rice (see Sushi Rice recipe)	4 cups

Filling:

chopped, sashimi quality raw tuna	7 oz
mayonnaise	3 Tbs
chili paste	1½ Tbs
sesame oil	½ tsp
sugar	½ tsp
dried nori seaweed (7" x 8" pieces)	4 sheets

Directions:

(1) In a bowl, mix all the filling ingredients and set aside.

(2) Place the bamboo rolling mat on a flat working surface. Place the nori on the bamboo rolling mat and spread one cup of the rice evenly over the nori by pressing with wet fingertips. Leave a one-inch border at the edge of the nori furthest from you. Spread the filling mixture in a half-inch wide line across the middle of the rice. Roll the sushi mat to make a tight roll.

(3) Allow each roll to rest for a minute before gently unrolling.

(4) Cut into 1½-inch long pieces. Repeat procedure for remaining rolls.

Alaskan Roll

(Serves 4)
Cooking Time: 20 minutes

Ingredients:

sushi rice (see Sushi Rice recipe)	4 cups

Filling:

smoked salmon sliced into long strips	7 oz
avocado thinly sliced into long strips	½ medium sized
green onion thinly sliced in long strips	8 pieces
cucumber thinly sliced in long strips	¼ medium sized
dried nori seaweed (7" x 8")	4 sheets

Directions:

(1)   Place the bamboo rolling mat on a flat working surface. Place the nori on the bamboo rolling mat and spread one cup of the rice evenly over the nori by pressing with wet fingertips. Leave a one-inch border at the edge of the nori furthest from you. Lay one each of the filling ingredients across the center of the rice. Roll the sushi mat to make a tight roll.

(2)   Allow each roll to rest for a minute before gently unrolling.

(3)   Cut into 1½-inch long pieces. Repeat procedure for remaining rolls.

Philadelphia Roll

(Serves 4)
Cooking Time: 20 minutes

Ingredients:

sushi rice (see Sushi Rice recipe)	4 cups

Filling:

sashimi grade raw salmon cut into thin strips	7 oz
cream cheese cut into thin strips	3½ oz
onion thinly sliced or cucumber in thin strips	4-8 pieces
dried nori seaweed (7" x 8" pieces)	4 sheets

Directions:

(1)   Place the bamboo rolling mat on a flat working surface. Place the nori on the bamboo rolling mat and spread one cup of the rice evenly over the nori by pressing with wet fingertips. Leave a one-inch border at the edge of the nori furthest from you. Spread the filling mixture in a half-inch wide line across the middle of the rice. Roll the sushi mat to make a tight roll.

(2)   Allow each roll to rest for a minute before gently unrolling.

(3)   Cut into 1½-inch long pieces. Repeat procedure for remaining rolls.

California Roll

(Serves 4)
Cooking Time: 20 minutes

Ingredients:

sushi rice (see Sushi Rice recipe)	4 cups

Filling:

avocado cut into thin strips	½ medium sized
crab meat (can be crab sticks) in thin strips	3½ oz
cucumber in thin strips	4-8 pieces
sesame seeds	to taste
dried nori seaweed (7" x 8" pieces)	4 sheets
sesame seeds for decoration	if desired

Directions:

(1) Cut a paper towel to the size of the dried nori seaweed. Place the paper towel on a bamboo rolling mat and place the nori on top. Spread one cup sushi rice evenly over the nori by pressing with wet finger tips.

(2) Flip the nori and rice over so the rice faces down. Lay the filling ingredients in a line along the middle of the nori.

(3) Hold the ingredients in place with your fingers and roll firmly.

(4) Allow each roll to rest for a minute and then gently unroll and remove the paper towel. Sprinkle with sesame seeds on the outside for decoration.

(5) Cut into 1½-inch long pieces. Repeat procedure for remaining rolls.

Seafood

魚

Mustard Panko Crusted Cod Fish

(Serves 4)

Cooking Time: 15 minutes

Cod is easy to find and has a clean taste, without any fishy or oily qualities, so it is a good fish to use if your family has finicky eaters. The panko crusted mustard flavor keeps it from being bland, without overwhelming the fish.

Ingredients:

codfish filets	4 pieces
whole grain Dijon mustard	4 tsp
red pepper	¼ medium sized
salt	to taste
olive oil	1 Tbs
lemon	for garnish

Seasoning:

panko*	6 Tbs
parsley	2 Tbs
olive oil	3 Tbs
salt	pinch
fresh black pepper	to taste

Directions:

(1) In a small bowl, mix all seasoning ingredients and set aside.

(2) Place the codfish filets on a plate and sprinkle with salt. In the baking pan for your toaster oven, place a sheet of aluminum foil and grease with olive oil.

(3) Evenly spread the mustard on both sides of the cod filets. Place filets side by side on the aluminum foil. Place the seasoning on top of the fish and put in oven toaster for 6-7 minutes until cooked.

(4) Cut the pepper into ¼-inch pieces. In a microwave safe bowl, add the pepper, a pinch of salt, and 1 tsp of the olive oil. Microwave on high without covering the bowl for 2 minutes.

(5) Serve the cod filets on a plate with lemon wedges and the red pepper on the side.

*Panko is Japanese for bread crumbs. Japanese bread crumbs are crispier and airier than Western bread crumbs, but if you can't find panko, use whatever is available.

Shrimp-Stuffed Shiitake Mushrooms

(Serves 4)
Cooking Time: 30 minutes

This makes great finger food and works well to serve as an appetizer at parties.

Ingredients:

fresh shiitake mushrooms	30 pieces
potato starch (katakuriko)	3 oz
shrimp—shelled and deveined	11 oz
bread crumbs	½ cup
vegetable oil	for deep frying
parsley	for garnish

Seasoning:

salt	1 tsp
ginger juice	2 tsp
sake	2 Tbs
sugar	2 tsp
egg white—beaten	1
cornstarch	¼ cup

Directions:

(1)   Grate ginger and press to extract 2 tsp of juice.

(2)   In a bowl, mix all seasoning ingredients.

(3)   To make the filling, remove the stems from the shiitake mushrooms and rinse with water. On a cutting board, finely chop the stems. Finely chop the shrimp until the texture becomes pasty. Add the shrimp and shiitake to the seasoning and mix well.

(4)   In a bowl, place the shiitake mushroom caps and coat both sides with Japanese potato starch. Stuff each cap with the filling. Press bread crumbs onto the top of each filled mushroom.

(5)   In a pan, heat the vegetable oil to 360°. Fry the mushrooms until the bread crumbs are nicely browned Remove from the oil and place on a paper towel to drain off the excess oil.

(6)   Arrange on a serving plate and garnish with the parsley.

Keiko's Easy Foil-Baked Whole Sea Bass

(Serves 4)

Cooking Time: 30 minutes

Recipes never include clean-up time, but as a busy woman, I know this is a factor when choosing what to make. This recipe significantly reduces clean-up time so when you're done, you can go watch your favorite TV show!

Ingredients:

whole sea bass	1
ginger—thinly sliced	1 1-inch knob
lemon rind—thinly sliced	1 medium size
green onion—finely chopped	½ bunch

Seasoning:

oyster sauce	3 Tbs
olive oil	1 Tbs
salt	to taste
pepper	to taste

Directions:

(1) In a shallow baking pan, place a sheet of aluminum foil large enough to form a pouch that will completely cover the sea bass. Place the whole fish on the aluminum foil and sprinkle with salt and pepper.

(2) Place the thinly sliced ginger, lemon rind, and finely chopped green onion on top of the sea bass. Pour the oyster sauce over the top and sprinkle with olive oil.

(3) Cover the fish with the foil and close the ends to make a pouch.

(4) Heat the oven to 325º and cook for 20 to 30 minutes until done.

Swordfish with Savory Ginger Soy Sauce

(Serves 4)

Cooking Time: 15 minutes

Ingredients:

swordfish filets	4 pieces
green onion finely chopped	2
lemon rinds	4 slices
tomatoes—wedged	2 small
flour	½ cup
vegetable oil	4 Tbs
salt	to taste
pepper	to taste

Sauce:

butter	2½ Tbs
ginger peeled and thinly shredded	2 1-inch knobs
white wine	4 Tbs
soy sauce	2 Tbs

Directions:

(1) To make the sauce, melt the butter in a small frying pan. Add the thinly shredded ginger and slowly sauté over low heat. Add the white wine and soy sauce to complete the sauce.

(2) Place the swordfish filets on a plate and sprinkle with salt and pepper on both sides. Lightly coat the filets with flour.

(3) Heat the vegetable oil in a frying pan and place the swordfish filets in pan, fry until both sides are nicely browned and cooked through.

(4) Serve on a plate with lemon rinds and finely chopped green onion on top. Pour the sauce on the fish. Serve with tomatoes on the side for garnish.

Yellowtail Teriyaki Donburi

(Serves 4)

Cooking Time: 20 minutes

This is one of my father's favorite home-cooked meals.

Ingredients:

yellowtail filets	4 pieces
green onion	for garnish
cooked Japanese short grain rice	4 cups

Sauce:

soy sauce	¼ cup
mirin*	2 Tbs
sugar	1 Tbs
lemon juice—freshly squeezed	1 medium-size

Directions:

(1) Sprinkle salt on the yellowtail filets. Let sit for 5 minutes, then remove any excess moisture by patting with a paper towel.

(2) While the fish is sitting, mix the ingredients for the sauce in a small bowl.

(3) Pour the sauce on the yellowtail filets. Let sit for 10 minutes.

(4) Spray a frying pan with olive oil or other vegetable oil, place the pan over medium heat. Place the marinated yellowtail filets and cook both sides. Using a pastry brush, brush the sauce over the fish continuously as you cook both sides.

(5) Serve in a bowl over rice and garnish on the top with the chopped green onion.

*Mirin is a Japanese rice wine, sweeter than sake. It helps reduce the fishy taste, though it should be used sparingly so as not to overpower the fish.

Herb Sautéd Yellowtail

(Serves 4)
Cooking Time: 15 minutes

This is a very rich and tasty dish that everybody enjoys.

Ingredients:

yellowtail filets	4 pieces
fresh pumpkin	1 small-sized
salt	to taste
pepper	to taste
olive oil	1 Tbs

Seasoning:

garlic—finely minced	2 cloves
parsley—finely chopped	5 Tbs
dill—finely chopped	5 Tbs
olive oil	1 Tbs

Directions:

(1) In a frying pan under medium heat, sauté the finely minced garlic in 1 Tbs of olive oil until lightly browned. Add the parsley and dill and toss with the garlic. When the herbs are moistened, season with salt and pepper. Remove from heat and set aside.

(2) Place the yellowtail filets on a plate and sprinkle with salt and pepper.

(3) Remove the seeds from the pumpkin and cut in half then slice thinly.

(4) Heat 1 Tbs of olive oil in a frying pan and saute the fish filets and the pumpkin slices turning each piece until the filets are browned on both sides and the pumpkin is throughly cooked.

(5) Serve on a plate with the seasoning spooned over the top of the yellowtail filets and with the pumpkin slices on the side.

Oysters in a Tangy, Spicy Sauce

(Serves 4)

Cooking Time: 25 minutes

This dish is a very traditional and most delicious way of eating oysters in Japan.

Ingredients:

fresh shelled oysters—rinsed and drained	16

Marinade:

sake	2 Tbs
soy sauce	1 Tbs

Sauce:

grated daikon radish	¼ cup
chili pepper paste	1 tsp
chopped leek	2 Tbs
lemon juice—freshly squeezed	2 medium-sized
soy sauce	1 Tbs
mirin*	1½ Tbs
parsley—finely chopped	2 Tbs

Directions:

(1) In a bowl, mix all sauce ingredients. Set aside.

(2) In another bowl, mix the mainade ingredients. Add the oysters and toss, making sure that the oysters are evenly covered in marinade. Let stand for 20 minutes.

(3) Heat a non-stick frying pan and cook the oysters over high heat until their shape becomes round and all sides are cooked.

(4) Place the oysters on individual serving plates and pour the sauce over them.

*Mirin is a Japanese rice wine, sweeter than sake. It helps reduce the fishy taste, though it should be used sparingly so as not to overpower the fish.

Tuna Tataki

(Serves 4)
Cooking Time: 20 minutes

This is one of the most popular dishes served in the Japanese restaurant.

Ingredients:

sashimi quality raw tuna	18 oz
lemon rind	8 slices
salt	to taste
pepper	to taste
vegetable oil	2 Tbs
ice water	1 quart

Sauce:

citrus soy sauce (ponzu)	2 Tbs
green onion finely chopped	5 Tbs
ginger juice	2 tsp
sliced onion	¼ cup

Directions:

(1) Grate ginger and press to extract 2 tsp of juice.
(2) In a small bowl, mix all sauce ingredients and set aside.
(3) Place the tuna on a plate and sprinkle with salt and pepper.
(4) Heat the vegtable oil in a frying pan over high heat and sear all sides of the tuna.
(5) Place the seared tuna in a shallow pan filled with the ice water. Make sure the tuna is covered completely. When the tuna has cooled, place it on a cutting board and remove excess moisture by patting it with a paper towel.
(6) Cut the tuna into ¼ inch slices and serve on a plate. Pour the sauce over the tuna and garnish with sliced lemon rind and chopped green onion.

Tri-Color Tuna Salad

(Serves 4)

Cooking Time: 15 minutes

Tuna and pineapple mixed together bring a harmonious marriage of flavors. This salad is made with simple ingredients yet is a restaurant-quality dish that serves to impress party-goers too.

Ingredients:

sashimi quality raw tuna	7 oz
avocado	2 medium-sized
pineapple	7 oz

Sauce:

mayonnaise	¼ cup
rice vinegar	3 Tbs
soy sauce	2 Tbs
salt	to taste
pepper	to taste
light vegetable oil	2 Tbs

Directions:

(1) In a bowl, mix all sauce ingredients and set aside.

(2) On a cutting board, cut the tuna, avocado, and pineapple into 1-inch pieces.

(3) Mix the tuna, avocado, and pineapple with the sauce and serve on a plate. If you want to be a little decorative, serve this salad in a carved-out pineapple. This makes a wonderful presentation for parties!

Tuna Carpaccio

(Serves 4)

Cooking Time: 20 minutes

This is an excellent dish to make as an appetizer.
It is nice and light and won't interfere with your entrée.

Ingredients:

sashimi quality raw tuna	18 oz
garlic	2 cloves
arugula	1 bunch
parmesan cheese—freshly grated	2 Tbs
olive oil	1 Tbs
salt	to taste
pepper	to taste

Sauce:

soy sauce	1 tsp
mayonnaise	¼ cup

Directions:

(1) In a small bowl mix the sauce ingredients.

(2) On a cutting board, slice the tuna into very thin slices. Thinly slice the garlic.

(3) Sauté the garlic over medium heat in 1 Tbs of olive oil. When the garlic begins to turn color, remove it from the pan and place on a paper towel to allow the excess oil to drain off.

(4) Break the arugula into bite-size pieces.

(5) Place the slices of tuna side by side on a plate and sprinkle with salt and pepper. Pour the sauce over the tuna and then top with arugula, garlic, and the parmesan cheese.

Salmon and Cauliflower in Curry

(Serves 4)

Cooking Time: 20 minutes

This is a interesting and tasty dish using curry as a flavoring. It is a very filling entrée.

Ingredients:

salmon filets	4 pieces
onion—thinly sliced	1 medium-size
cauliflower	1 head
carrot	1 small

Sauce:

butter	1 Tbs
white wine	¼ cup
water	1 cup
curry powder	2 tsp
fresh cream	1 cup
salt	to taste
pepper	to taste

Directions:

(1) Remove the thick stem of the cauliflower, divide the top into bite size pieces. Cut the carrot into strips ¼ inch wide and 2 inches long.

(2) Cut the salmon filets in half. Sprinkle with salt and pepper.

(3) In a frying pan, melt 1 Tbs of butter and sauté the onion slices. Add the salmon filets then pour in white wine and water. Add cauliflower and carrots and sprinkle curry powder on top. Bring the liquid to a boil, then set the heat to low and cover with lid. Cook for 10 minutes.

(4) Add fresh cream and just bring to a boil. Remove from the heat, season with salt and pepper and serve.

Keiko's Sweet and Sour Salmon

(Serves 4)

Cooking Time: 25 minutes

The sweet and sour taste with salmon is just simply delicious. Please try this dish!

Ingredients:

salmon filets	4 pieces
red and yellow bell pepper	¼ each
onion	1 medium
salt	to taste
potato starch (katakuriko)	2 tsp
vegetable oil	1 Tbs
sake	2 Tbs
vegetable oil	for frying

Sauce:

rice vinegar	1 Tbs
sugar	1 Tbs
chicken stock	2 cubes
hot water	1 cup
salt	to taste
potato starch (katakuriko)	2 tsp
water	2 tsp

Directions:

(1) In a bowl, mix first 5 sauce ingredients and set aside.

(2) Sprinkle the salmon filets with salt and the sake on both sides. Let sit for 5 minutes.

(3) Thinly slice the onion and peppers.

(4) Remove any excess moisture from the salmon filets by patting with a paper towel. Lightly coat with potato starch on both sides. Set aside.

(5) In a frying pan, heat the oil to 360º and fry the salmon filets until cooked. Remove the filets from the oil and let any excess oil drip off.

(6) Sauté the onion and peppers in 1 Tbs vegetable oil, then add the sauce and warm over high heat.

(7) Mix 2 tsp of starch and 2 tsp of water and add this to the sauce to thicken it.

(8) Place the salmon filets on plates and pour the sauce-vegetable mixture on top.

Easy Yellowtail Teriyaki

(Serves 4)

Cooking Time: 15 minutes

This is a most popular item being served in the Japanese restaurants in the United States.

Ingredients:

yellowtail filets	4 pieces
broccoli	1 head
vegetable oil	2 Tbs

Sauce:

sugar	2 Tbs
sake	3 Tbs
mirin*	3 Tbs
soy sauce	5 Tbs
salt	to taste

Directions:

(1)   In a frying pan, add all the sauce ingredients. Bring to a boil, then remove from the heat and set aside.

(2)   Sauté the broccoli in 1 Tbs of vegetable oil. Season with salt.

(3)   Add the remaining vegetable oil to another frying pan and heat until it begins to smoke. Over medium heat, place the yellowtail filets in the pan with skin side down. Turn and fry both sides until cooked. Make sure to shake the pan to prevent sticking.

(4)   Remove any excess oil from the frying pan and bring the heat to medium high. Add the sauce and cook until the sauce evenly covers the yellowtail filets. Make sure you continue to shake the frying pan frequently to prevent sticking. When the sauce is thickened, remove from the heat. Serve the fillets on a plate with the broccoli on the side.

*Mirin is a Japanese rice wine, sweeter than sake. It helps reduce the fishy taste, though it should be used sparingly so as not to overpower the fish.

Garlic-Fried Salmon Salad

(Serves 4)
Cooking Time: 15 minutes

This is a very filling salad that can be served as a main course.

Ingredients:

salmon filets	4 pieces
garlic—grated	½ clove
dill	1 bunch (or 1 small package)
watercress	3 bunches
radicchio	8 leaves
flour	½ cup
salt	to taste
vegetable oil	for frying

Dressing:

lemon juice	2 Tbs
olive oil	6 Tbs
salt	1 tsp
capers	2 Tbs
pepper	to taste

Directions:

(1) In a bowl, mix all dressing ingredients and set aside.

(2) Cut the salmon filets at an angle into ¼-inch thick slices. Sprinkle with salt , pepper and garlic. Press the garlic onto the fish with your fingertips.

(3) Place the salmon filets on a plate and lightly coat them with flour.

(4) Heat the vegetable oil for frying in a pan to 365° and fry the fish for 1 to 2 minutes until cooked.

(5) Using your fingers, break the dill and radicchio into bite size pieces. Break the watercress into 2½-inch long pieces.

(6) Toss the fried fish, dill, watercress, and radicchio together and place on individual serving dishes. Add the dressing over the top.

Foiled Miso Salmon

(Serves 4)

Cooking Time: 20 minutes

Anyone who loves the flavor of miso will go crazy over this dish!

Ingredients:

salmon filets	4 pieces
green onion	2 sprigs
shiitake mushrooms	8

Marinade:

miso	3 Tbs
mirin*	2 Tbs
sake	2 Tbs
soy sauce	2 tsp
sugar	1 Tbs
red pepper flakes (shichimi togarashi)	for garnish

Directions:

(1)   In a bowl mix all marinade ingredients.

(2)   Cut the salmon into bite size pieces.

(3)   In a shallow pan, place the fish and add the marinade. Marinate for 10 minutes.

(4)   Thinly slice the green onion at an angle. Remove the stems from the shiitake mushrooms and cut the tops in half.

(5)   Preheat an oven to 400 degrees.

(6)   In a baking pan place a sheet of aluminum foil long enough to make a pouch. Place the ingredients on the foil in the following order: green onion on the bottom, marinated salmon, and shiitake on top. Fold in the sides and ends of the aluminum foil to make a pouch, make sure to seal tightly so that the juices won't flow out.

(7)   Place inside the oven for 7 to 8 minutes or until done. Sprinkle with Japanese hot pepper flakes.

*Mirin is a Japanese rice wine, sweeter than sake. It helps reduce the fishy taste, though it should be used sparingly so as not to overpower the fish.

Chinese-Style Flavorful Salmon

(Serves 4)

Cooking Time: 15 minutes

Though typically salmon dishes are matched with cream sauces, salmon enjoys a wonderful harmony with the Chinese style sauce in this dish. By using this recipe you'll find a whole new way of enjoying this popular fish.

Ingredients:

salmon filets with skin	4 pieces
cilantro sprigs	for garnish
flour	¼ cup
salt	1 tsp
vegetable oil	2 Tbs

Sauce:

soy sauce	2 Tbs
rice vinegar	1½ Tbs
sugar	1½ tsp
sesame oil	1½ tsp
green onion—finely chopped	2 sprigs
ginger—finely minced	1 1-inch knob
garlic—finely minced	1 clove

Directions:

(1)   In a bowl, mix all the sauce ingredients.

(2)   Cut the salmon into bite size pieces and sprinkle with 1 tsp of salt and let sit for 5 minutes. Remove any excess moisture from the fish by patting with paper towels. Lightly coat the fish with flour, shaking off excess flour.

(3)   Heat the vegetable oil in a frying pan. Over medium heat, fry both sides of the fish for 2 to 3 minutes on each side until the salmon skin becomes crispy.

(4)   Pour off excess oil from the frying pan. Add the sauce and fold the sauce over until the fish is evenly coated.

(5)   Serve, garnishing the dishes with the cilantro.

Keiko's Everyday Miso Cod

(Serves 4)

Cooking Time: 20 minutes

Any Japanese food enthusiast must have had this dish at least once as it is one of the most-ordered dishes in Japanese restaurants. However making miso cod at home, using the typical recipe, is time-consuming as you have to marinate it overnight. Here I offer you an easy way to duplicate this dish and be able to serve it right away!

Ingredients:

codfish filets	4 pieces
vegetable oil	for frying
mirin*	½ cup
basil leaves—fresh	for garnish

Sauce:

miso	½ cup
mirin	¼ cup
peanut butter	1 Tbs
soy sauce	1 Tbs
sugar	¼ cup
sake	¼ cup

Directions:

(1) In a saucepan, add sake and heat to evaporate the alcohol content. Add remaining sauce ingredients and continue heating over low heat. Do not bring to boil.

(2) In a shallow pan, place the fish and add ½ cup of mirin. Marinate for 10 minutes.

(3) Heat the oil in a frying pan and fry the cod filets until cooked evenly on both sides, about 2 to 3 minutes a side.

(4) Serve hot on individual plates and pour the sauce over the fish. Garnish with the fresh basil leaves.

*Mirin is a Japanese rice wine, sweeter than sake. It helps reduce the fishy taste, though it should be used sparingly so as not to overpower the fish.

Favorite Seafood Tempura

(Serves 4)

Cooking Time: 25 minutes

Tempura is one of the favorite dishes in my family and with many Americans who enjoy Japanese food. For people who don't like seafood and vegetables prepared in other ways, this is a great way to make it enjoyable!

Ingredients:

shrimp	8 medium-sized
white fish	4 pieces
shiitake mushrooms	8
kabocha pumpkin	1 small

Batter for Seafood

Tip: Make sure to use ice-cold water for crispy batter!

egg	1 medium-sized
ice water	1 cup
flour	¾ cup
cornstarch	¼ cup
baking powder	1 tsp

Dipping Sauce:

mirin	¼ cup
soy sauce	¼ cup
dashi stock	1 cup
grated daikon radish	¼ cup

Directions:

(1) In a bowl, mix together dipping sauce ingredients and set aside.

(2) Remove the stem of the shiitake mushroom. Kabocha pumpkin should be thinly sliced into pieces one-third-inch in thickness.

(3) Using deep iron pan, add vegetable oil for frying and bring to 330º. Note that if the oil is below 285º, the batter will sink to the bottom of the pan, above 375º, the batter will float to the surface. Maintain the oil's temperature as close to 330º as possible.

(4) Dip the ingredients in the batter and place a few ingredients at a time into the heated oil. Do not add too many at once as this will force the temperature to drop.

(5) When the surface turns crispy golden brown, remove from oil to a wire rack and let excess oil drip off.

(6) Serve the tempura with lemon wedge garnish and the dipping sauce on the side.

Meat

牛肉

Beef

鶏肉

Chicken

豚肉

Pork

Sukiyaki

(Serves 4)

Cooking Time: 25 minutes

Sukiyaki is familiar to several generations of Americans. It brings back memories of meals with my family as it is one of my father's favorite dishes. This is a great dish to make for your family or for friends, as sharing from one pan is a very intimate and fun-filled experience!

Ingredients:

thinly sliced beef	30 oz
tofu—firm	1 12-oz package
shiitake mushrooms	8 pieces
eringi mushrooms	2
green onion	2 sprigs
spinach	1 bunch
eggs—lightly beaten	4 medium
sesame oil	2 Tbs

Sauce:

sake	1 cup
mirin	½ cup
soy sauce	½ cup
sugar	3 Tbs

Broth:

dashi stock	2-3 cups

Directions:

(1) In a small pot over medium heat, mix all sauce ingredients, cook for 3 to 4 minutes, bring to boil then remove from heat and set aside.

(2) Cut off the stems of shiitake mushrooms and cut them in half. For eringi, cut off the tip of the stem and cut the mushroom lengthwise into long strips.

(3) Cut the tofu into 6 to 8 even-sized pieces and slice the green onion diagonally into 1-inch thicknesses. Cut the spinach into two-inch long pieces.

(4) Put the sesame oil in a sukiyaki style pan, or if you don't have one, a deep frying pan. Place on medium heat. Once the oil is heated, add shiitake and eringi and sauté. Once the mushrooms are cooked, add half of the sauce. Bring liquid to a boil.

(5) Add the beef, tofu and green onion in that order. Pour in half of the dashi stock and cook over medium heat for 3 to 4 minutes. Add the spinach and cook until done, about 2 to 3 minutes.

(6) In each of four small bowls, lightly beat 1 egg. Each diner gets a bowl.

(7) Place the pan in the center of the table. Using chopsticks or a fork each person helps himself, one portion at a time, dipping each portion in the egg.

(8) Add the remaining dashi stock and sauce when the liquid in the pan gets low.

Beef and Scallion Sauté
with Fresh Black Pepper

(Serves 4)

Cooking Time: 10 minutes

This dish can be made so quickly that it's perfect for when you don't have much time. It's also a great meat entrée for meat lovers.

Ingredients:

thinly sliced beef	14 oz
scallions	2
two different kinds of mushrooms	4 oz each
butter	1 Tbs
sake	1 cup
freshly ground black pepper	to taste

Directions:

(1) Cut the scallions diagonally to 1-inch thickness.

(2) Cut the beef into bite size pieces. For the mushrooms, remove the stems and cut into bite size pieces.

(3) In a frying pan, melt the butter over medium heat. Once the butter is melted, add the beef and sauté until it changes color.

(4) Add scallions and mushrooms. Add the sake and black pepper and continue cooking until the meat is done, about 3 to 4 minutes.

Rocky's Special Wasabi Steak

(Serves 4)

Cooking Time: 15 minutes

Rocky loves steak and this is how he prefers to have it. Some steak sauces overwhelm the flavor of the steak, but this combination of wasabi, butter, and soy sauce creates a harmonious combination. Once you eat steak served this way, it's the only way you'll want to eat steak again.

Ingredients:

beef filets—4 oz each	4
vegetable oil	2 Tbs
butter	4 pats
salt	to taste
pepper	to taste

Sauce:

wasabi	1 Tbs
mirin	3 Tbs
soy sauce	½ Tbs
sake	1 Tbs
sesame oil	1 tsp

Directions:

(1)   In a small bowl, mix the sauce ingredients.

(2)   Sprinkle salt and pepper on the beef.

(3)   Heat the vegetable oil in a frying pan and add the beef filets. Cook both sides evenly to your liking.

(4)   Pour the sauce over the filets.

(5)   Place a pat of butter on top of each filet.

All Time Favorite Beef with Asparagus

(Serves 4)

Cooking Time: 25 minutes

In Japanese restaurants, scallions are used for this dish rather than the asparagus that I suggest. This recipe is easier and just as flavorful. You can also use string beans instead of asparagus.

Ingredients:

thinly sliced beef	8-12 slices
asparagus	10 to 15 spears
flour	3 Tbs
vegetable oil	2 Tbs
salt	to taste

Sauce:

soy sauce	3 Tbs
mirin	3 Tbs
sake	3 Tbs
water	3 Tbs

Directions:

(1) In a small bowl, mix all sauce ingredients and set aside.

(2) Boil the water in a pan, drop in asparagus and cook halfway. Remove from water.

(3) Roll each slice of beef diagonally around two or three asparagus spears.

(4) Sprinkle the flour in the bottom of a shallow pan or flat plate. Evenly coat the rolled beef and asparagus with the flour. Pat off excess flour.

(5) Heat the vegetable oil in a frying pan over medium heat. Place the rolled beef with asparagus side by side in the pan and fry, turning the pieces until all sides are done.

(6) Cut rolled asparagus into thirds. Replace into pan.

(7) Add the sauce and heat over medium heat. When the sauce begins to reduce, remove from the frying pan and serve on plates.

Eggplant and Beef Sauté with Miso

(Serves 4)

Cooking Time: 15 minutes

The enzyme in the miso softens the beef, making it more digestible.

Ingredients:

Japanese eggplant	2 medium-sized
beef	4 oz
green onion—with stalk	1
garlic—finely minced	2 cloves
vegetable oil	2 Tbs
sesame oil	1 tsp
salted water	1 quart
salt and pepper	to taste

Sauce:

miso	3 Tbs
sugar	4 tsp
sake	2 Tbs
soy sauce	2 Tbs

Directions:

(1)   In a small bowl, mix all sauce ingredients and set aside.

(2)   On a cutting board, remove the eggplant stem and cut lengthwise into long strips. Soak stips in salted water. Cut the green onion diagonally into ¼-inch thicknesses.

(3)   Cut the beef into bite-size pieces and sprinkle with salt and pepper.

(4)   Drain the eggplant and pat dry with a paper towel.

(5)   Heat the vegetable oil and sesame oil in a frying pan. Add the finely minced garlic. When the garlic becomes aromatic, add green onion, beef, and the eggplant. Gently turn the beef mixture until the oil is evenly distributed throughout. Add the sauce to the pan and cook until done to your liking.

Shabu Shabu Salad

(Serves 4)

Cooking Time: 15 minutes

For this to be successful, always use beef that is well marbleized. It is much tastier, and yet still healthy since this is basically a salad.

Ingredients:

thinly sliced beef	30 oz
cucumber—peeled and thinly sliced	1 medium-sized
watercress	1 bunch
onion—thinly sliced	1 medium-sized
sesame seeds	for garnish

Sauce:

tahini	3 Tbs
soy sauce	¼ cup
vinegar	1 Tbs
sugar	3 Tbs
green onion—finely chopped	1 Tbs
ginger—finely minced	1 Tbs
garlic—finely minced	1 Tbs

Directions:

(1) In a bowl, mix together the sauce ingredients.

(2) Drop the sliced beef Into a pot of boiling water and cook to desired doneness.

(3) On a plate, arrange the cucumber, watercress, and onion. Place the cooked beef in the center and pour the sauce over the beef. Sprinkle with sesame seeds if desired.

Beef and Daikon Country Style Soup

(Serves 4)

Cooking Time: 30 minutes

This is a perfect soup for an especially cold winter's day because it gives you an earthy, warm feeling inside.

Ingredients:

beef—thinly sliced	18 oz
Japanese daikon radish	2 cups
black pepper	1 Tbs
water	4 cups

Marinade:

soy sauce	3 Tbs
garlic—grated	2 cloves

Directions:

(1)   In a shallow pan, mix together marinade ingredients and marinate the beef.

(2)   Peel the daikon radish and cut width-wise into thin slices. Cut each of these pieces into 4 fan-shaped pieces.

(3)   In a pan, bring water to boil and add the daikon radish.

(4)   Add the beef and sprinkle with black pepper. Cook until done.

Chicken and Egg Over Rice

(Serves 4)
Cooking Time: 15 minutes.

I can't help thinking of my home in Tokyo and my mother when I think of this dish.
To a Japanese, this is true comfort food.

Ingredients:

boneless chicken leg and thigh	1 each
onion	1 medium
eggs—lightly beaten	4 medium
spinach	10 sprigs
California white rice—cooked	3 cups

Stock:

salt	1 tsp
soy sauce	2 tsp
mirin	1½ tsp
dashi	2 cups

Directions:

(1) Mix the stock ingredients in a bowl.

(2) Thinly slice the onion. Cut the chicken into bite-size pieces.

(3) Pour the stock into a small frying pan, add the chicken and onion and cook until done, about 5 minutes. Pour the lightly beaten eggs slowly on top the chicken and onion. Add the spinach and cover the pan with a lid. Simmer until the egg is almost set.

(4) Divide the rice evenly into 4 bowls (preferably domburi bowls, which are large enough for each portion). Place the cooked chicken and egg on top of the rice.

Juicy Tatsuta-Style Fried Chicken

(Serves 4)

Cooking Time: 20 minutes

I often double the ingredients when making this dish because it is good both hot and cold, so it's good for leftovers. It's also a must if I'm preparing food for a picnic.

Ingredients:

boneless chicken breast	4 pieces
lemon wedges	for garnish
potato starch (katakuriko)	½ cup
vegetable oil	for deep frying

Marinade

ginger juice	1 Tbs
sake	3 Tbs
soy sauce	¼ cup

Directions:

(1) Grate the ginger and press to extract 1 Tbs of juice.

(2) In a bowl, mix the marinade ingredients and set aside.

(3) Cut the chicken into bite-size pieces.

(4) Toss the chicken in the marinade and marinate for 20 minutes.

(5) Remove the chicken and let any excess marinade drip off. Coat the chicken with the potato starch.

(6) Heat the oil in a pan to 340º. Deep fry the chicken pieces until cooked, about 5 minutes. After frying, place the chicken on a paper towel to remove extra oil. Place on a plate and garnish with lemon wedges.

Keiko's Original Oven-Baked Chicken Yakitori

Cooking Time: 30 minutes
(Serves 4)

The traditional way to make chicken yakitori is is to grill it over charcoal,
but to simplify your life, I created an easy oven-baked style.
This dish is one of the most popular bar foods in Japan.

Ingredients:

boneless chicken breast	4 pieces
bamboo skewers	

Marinade:

sugar	2 Tbs
sake	2 Tbs
soy sauce	6 Tbs
ginger juice	2 Tbs

Directions:

(1)   Preheat the oven to 400º.

(2)   Grate ginger and press to extract 2 Tbs of juice.

(3)   In a medium bowl, place mix the marinade ingredients.

(4)   Cut the chicken into bite-size pieces.

(5)   Add the chicken to the marinade and marinate for 10 minutes.

(6)   Skewer the chicken pieces and place the skewers on a greased baking pan. Bake for 20 minutes.

(7)   When the chicken is done, place the chicken on a plate to serve.

Healthy Steamed Chicken and Eggplant with Hot Spicy Sauce

(Serves 4)

Cooking Time: 25 minutes

When you don't have much of appetite, this is a perfect dish because the hot-spicy flavor will entice you into digging in every time.

Ingredients:

boneless chicken thighs	4 pieces
Japanese eggplant	8 pieces
sake	1½ Tbs

Sauce:

green onion	1 stalk
ginger	2 1-inch knobs
cilantro—finely chopped	8 sprigs
hot red pepper—finely chopped	3 pieces
rice vinegar	6 Tbs
sugar	6 Tbs
soy sauce	3 Tbs

Directions:

(1) Chop the ginger and onion into small pieces. In a bowl, mix the sauce ingredients.

(2) Peel the eggplant and cut it into 1-inch cubes.

(3) Place the chicken and eggplant in a shallow pan and sprinkle with 1½ Tbs of sake.

(4) Place a paper baking sheet (optional) inside a steamer. Make sure that the steamer is heated before placing the sheet inside.

(5) Place the chicken and eggplant side by side inside the steamer and cook until chicken is done and the eggplant is soft, about 15 minutes.

(6) Cut the chicken in bite-size pieces, mix with the eggplant and pour the sauce over the top.

Japanese-Style Juicy Chicken Meat Balls

(Serves 4)

Cooking Time: 25 minutes

*T*his is a typical meal to put in a child's lunchbox, and I remember it well from those days. But adults love it also, especially Japanese adults for whom it brings back such fond memories.

Ingredients:

ground chicken	21 oz
green onion—finely chopped	1½
ginger—finely diced	½ 1-inch knob
panko (bread crumbs)	½ cup
salt	1 tsp
sake	2 Tbs
flour	2 Tbs
vegetable oil	2 Tbs

Sauce:

soy sauce	¼ cup
mirin	¼ cup
water	¼ cup

Directions:

(1) In a small bowl, mix the sauce ingredients and set aside.

(2) Place the chicken, onion, ginger, bread crumbs, salt, and sake in a separate bowl. Using your hand, blend well.

(3) Take about one-twelfth of the mixture in your hand and gently pat it 2 or 3 times to take the air out. Shape it into an oval. Continue making the same shapes with remaining mixture. I recommend you make them small as it's easier to eat and easy to cook.

(4) Coat all sides of the oval shaped pieces with flour. By covering the pieces with the flour, the juice from the chicken will remain sealed inside and the sauce will cover the pieces thoroughly.

(5) Heat the oil over a medium heat and place the chicken pieces in it. Fry, turning, until all sides are browned. Pour the sauce over the chicken and shake the pan to make sure that the sauce is spread evenly.

(6) Place a lid over the top and let simmer over medium heat for 3 minutes. Once the chicken pieces are done, remove the lid and turn the heat to high to evaporate the water and thicken the sauce. Once the sauce is thick and mixed well with the chicken pieces, remove the chicken from the pan and place on a plate. Pour remaining sauce over the chicken.

Exotic Chicken and
Spinach with Mustard Sauce

Serves 4
Cooking Time: 20 minutes

You can use this same recipe without the chicken to create a tasty vegetarian dish.

Ingredients:

spinach	½ bunch
bean sprouts with beans	½ bag
red bell pepper	1 medium
chicken breast	1 large

Sauce:

vegetable oil	1 Tbs
sesame oil	1 Tbs
vinegar	2 Tbs
soy sauce	2 Tbs
sugar	1 Tbs
Japanese yellow mustard (karashi)	2 tsp
French mustard with seeds	2 tsp
pepper	to taste

Seasoning:

ginger—thinly sliced	1 1-inch knob
salt	to taste
bay leaf	1 leaf

Directions:

(1)   In a bowl, mix sauce ingredients and set aside.

(2)   Cut the spinach into 2-inch pieces. Remove the roots of the bean sprouts and remove the seeds from the red pepper and thinly slice it.

(3)   In a small pot, bring 2 to 3 cups of water to boil and add the seasoning ingredients. Then add the chicken and cook until done, about 5 minutes. Remove the chicken from the pot and let it cool. Do not throw away the water from the pot that was used to cook the chicken, set it aside.

(4)   Using the same water add spinach, red pepper, and bean sprouts and cook on medium heat for a few minutes. Remove the vegetables from the pot and strain.

(5)   Once the chicken is cooled, break it into bite size pieces with your fingers.

(6)   Mix the chicken, vegetables, and the sauce and it's ready to serve.

Healthy Soba Salad

*T*his is a great salad to take for lunch. I bring it to the office frequently.
It's very good for those who enjoy Japanese cuisine, and also very healthy.

Ingredients:

mixed greens	1 6-oz bag
buckwheat noodles	1 12-oz package
boneless chicken breast—cooked and	
cut into thin strips	1 breast
cherry tomatoes	12
dried seaweed (nori)	for garnish

Dressing:

soba dipping sauce	½ cup
wasabi	1 tsp
vinegar	½ cup
vegetable oil	¼ cup

Directions:

(1)　In a small bowl, mix dressing ingredients and set aside.

(2)　Cut dried seaweed into thin stips using scissors.

(2)　Boil water in a deep pan and cook the buckwheat noodles until soft. Quickly remove the cooked buckwheat noodles from the hot water and place them into cold running water. Drain then cut the cool noodles into 4-inch long pieces with a knife.

(3)　Place the mixed greens, tomatoes, and chicken with the noodles on a plate. Sprinkle with seaweed and pour dressing over top.

Ginger Pork (Shogayaki)

(Serves 4)
Cooking Time: 10 minutes

Pork is a good and leaner alternative to red meat. Ginger pork is one of the classic staples of Japanese home cooking. This dish is also known as one of the top five picks of Japanese men when asked to name their favorite home-cooked meal.

Ingredients:

pork loin—thinly sliced like bacon strips	21 oz
onions	3 medium
vegetable oil	3 Tbs
salt	to taste

Sauce:

soy sauce	5 Tbs
ginger juice	2 Tbs
sake	2 Tbs
sugar	2 Tbs

Directions:

(1) Grate the ginger and press to extract 2 Tbs of juice. Mix all the sauce ingredients in a small bowl and set aside.

(2) Cut the onions in half lengthwise and then slice into half moons ½ inch wide. Cutting the onions in this shape will allow the sliced pork to mix well with the onions.

(3) Place the thinly sliced pork in a shallow baking pan and sprinkle evenly with salt.

(4) Heat the vegetable oil in a frying pan over high heat and sauté the pork slices on one side until each is a light brown color then turn and sauté on other side to the same light brown color.

(5) Once all the meat is lightly browned, add the onions.

(6) When the onions become transparent, add the sauce and mix.

(7) Continue to cook the meat, onions, and sauce on medium to high heat until the sauce thickens. Once the sauce thickens and is evenly mixed with the pork and the onion, the dish is ready.

(8) Serve on a plate with your favorite side vegetable such as steamed broccoli or fresh tomatoes.

Pork Cutlets with Sweet Miso Sauce

(Serves 4)

Cook Time: 30 minutes

Pork cutlets alone can be bit bland, but I find pork and miso is a great taste combination. You will feel very satisfied with this meal. This is one of my husband Rocky's favorite meals. Miso helps you to digest the food too, so I'd really love for you to try this dish!

Ingredients:

pork loin chops (thin)	2 lbs
eggs	2 medium
milk	2 Tbs
white flour	½ cup
Japanese panko (bread crumbs)	1 cup
salt	to taste
pepper	to taste
cabbage—shredded	2 cups
vegetable oil	for frying

Sauce:

miso	1 cup
sugar	10 Tbs
mirin	¼ cup
water	6 Tbs

Directions:

(1) In a small saucepan, mix the sauce ingredients and cook over low heat, stirring with a wooden spoon. The sauce is done when it has a cake batter-like thickness. Once the sauce is ready, set it aside.

(2) Score the fat on the pork with a sharp knife. Tenderize the pork by pounding it with a flat meat mallet. Sprinkle with salt and pepper.

(3) Beat the eggs and milk in a bowl.

(4) Coat both sides of the pork cutlets in the flour and then dip them in the beaten eggs. Coat both sides of the pork with bread crumbs.

(5) In a pan, heat the frying oil to 350º and fry the pork chops until the bread crumbs are well browned.

(6) Cut the fried pork cutlets to your desired size and place on a plate. Add shredded cabbage as a side garnish. Pour the sauce over the cutlets.

Fried Pork and Cucumber with Sweet Tomato Sauce

(Serves 4)
Cook Time: 20 minutes

This dish is similar to sweet and sour pork. Though it's made from simple items found in your refrigerator, by being creative with them, you'll be serving a dish to your family that will look like it came from a top chef. This dish is so delicious that you'll want to make it again the next day!

Ingredients:

leg of pork—sliced like bacon strips	14 oz
cucumber—kirby type recommended	4
potato starch (katakuriko)	¼ cup
vegetable oil	¼ cup

Sauce:

ketchup	10 Tbs
vinegar	5 tsp
sugar	¼ cup
soy sauce	2 tsp

Marinade:

ginger & juice, peeled and grated	1 1-inch knob
sake	1 Tbs
soy sauce	2 tsp

Directions:

(1) In a bowl, mix the sauce ingredients and set aside.

(2) Grate the ginger and press to extract juice. Mix with rest of marinade ingredients and set aside.

(3) Cut the pork strips into bite-size pieces. Mix with the marinade and marinate for 10 minutes.

(4) Cut the cucumber into ½ inch to 1 inch thick pieces. Use a paper towel to pat off any excess water.

(5) Heat the frying oil in a pan to 340º. Coat the pork strips with the starch and place them in the oil. Turn the pork over to make sure that both sides are evenly fried. After the pork is done, quickly fry the cucumber.

(6) Mix the fried pork strips and cucumber, place on a plate and pour the sauce over the meat.

YELLOW
PEACH
$2⁰⁰/lb

Vegetable/Tofu

野菜

Vegetable

豆腐

Tofu

Baby Shrimp with Edamame

(Serves 4)

Cooking Time: 20 minutes

This dish makes a very simple, yet very flavorful entrée. Goes well with steamed white rice. Edamame is quite healthy for you, and is known for supporting longevity.

Ingredients:

edamame, cooked and removed from the pod	1 cup
shrimp, peeled	¼ cup
green onion—finely minced	1 stalk
vegetable oil	2 Tbs
vegetable oil	for frying
baby romaine lettuce	

Marinade:

sake	¼ cup
potato starch (katakuriko)	1 tsp

Seasoning:

sake	1 Tbs
sugar	1 tsp
salt	1 tsp
pepper	to taste

Direction:

(1)   In a bowl, mix marinade ingredients, add shrimp and set aside to marinate.

(2)   In a pot, bring water to boil. Add salt and cook the edamame. When cooked, drain and set aside.

(3)   Heat the vegetable oil to 300° and fry the shrimp until it begins to have color—don't turn your back, shrimp doesn't take very long to cook. Drip off any excess oil and set cooked shrimp aside.

(4)   In a pan, heat 2 Tbs of vegetable oil and sauté the minced green onion. Add the cooked edamame and the seasoning ingredients.

(5)   Add the shrimp to the pan and sauté all the ingredients together for a minute or two. If you want, add butter for an added savory flavor. Serve over romaine lettuce leaves.

Edamame Kanoko

(Serves 4)
Cooking Time: 25 minutes

Many Americans are familiar with edamame as a salty appetizer, but this dish allows you to enjoy edamame in a heartier fashion.

Ingredients:

edamame—removed from the pod	½ cup
ham	2 slices
onion finely chopped	½ medium-sized
corn kernels	½ cup
flour	¼ cup
vegetable oil	for frying

Batter:

egg yolk	1
flour	1 cup
ice water	11 oz

Sauce:

mirin	3 Tbs
soy sauce	3 Tbs
dashi stock	1 cup

Make sure that you use ice-cold water to make the batter.
This is important to make a successful tempura!

Directions:

(1) In a small pot, mix the sauce ingredients and bring to a boil. Remove from heat and set aside.

(2) In a pot, bring water to boil, put loose edamame beans in the water and return to a boil. Cook for 2 to 3 minutes then remove from heat and drain.

(3) Cut the onion and the ham in ½-inch cubes.

(4) In a bowl, add edamame, onion, ham, and corn. Sprinkle with flour and mix well.

(5) Place batter ingredients in a bowl and blend well. Add the edamame-ham mixture and toss well to coat with the batter evenly.

(6) In a deep pan, heat vegetable oil to 350°. Using a soup spoon, add dollops of the batter mix. Don't make the dollops too large, no bigger than the size of your palm. Fry until cooked to a light brown, remove from the oil with tongs and allow excess oil to drip off.

(7) Serve on a plate with sauce in a small dipping bowl on the side.

Keiko's Spicy Dynamite Edamame

(Serves 4)

Cooking Time: 10 minutes

This is great party food; pairs perfectly with wine and beer. Be careful not to drink too much as this dish and the beverages go together really well!

Ingredients:

edamame pods	2 cups

Sauce:

vegetable oil	¼ cup
chili powder	2 Tbs
garlic powder	2 Tbs
salt	2 tsp

Directions:

(1)   In a bowl, mix all sauce ingredients and set aside.

(2)   Steam the edamame for 3 to 5 minutes to cook. Remove from heat and allow to cool.

(3)   In a separate, serving bowl, place the cooked edamame and mix with the sauce.

Virgin Tofu

(Serves 4)
Cooking Time: 8 minutes

If you've had a hard day and get home late, what should you eat? Having a big meal right before going to bed is unhealthy. This dish is not only very popular in Japan, and takes almost no time to prepare, but it will also satisfy your appetite without leaving you with a full belly at bedtime.

Ingredients:

firm tofu (momen tofu)	2 12-oz packages
onion	1 large
salt	to taste
parsley or chili powder	for garnish

Seasoning:

sesame oil	2 Tbs
soy sauce	2 Tbs
sugar	2 tsp

Directions:

(1)   In a small bowl, mix seasoning ingredients.

(2)   Cut the tofu into 1-inch cubes.

(3)   Thinly slice the onion. Sprinkle with salt and mix well with your hands. Let it sit for 5 minutes. Pat off the excess moisture from the onion with a water-soaked paper towel.

(4)   Place the thinly sliced onion in a small bowl and mix with seasonings.

(5)   Place the cubed tofu on a plate and serve onion mixture over the top. Garnish with parsley or sprinkle some chili powder.

Tofu Steak with Creamy Mushroom Sauce

(Serves 4)

Cooking Time: 15 minutes

For anyone who thinks tofu is bland and can't fill you up, this dish will prove that tofu can be transformed into a hearty and satisfying entrée. This is one of my vegetarian friends' favorite dishes.

Ingedients:

firm tofu (momen tofu)	2 cakes
white mushrooms	½ lbs
vegetable oil	2 Tbs
butter	4 Tbs

Seasoning:

soy sauce	1 Tbs
potato starch (katakuriko)	1 Tbs
water	1 Tbs

Sauce:

soy sauce	1 Tbs
white wine	3 Tbs
fresh cream	3 Tbs
salt and pepper	to taste

Directions:

(1) Cut the tofu in half, wrap it with a paper towel, and place on a plate. Microwave for 1 minute on high to remove excess moisture.

(2) In a bowl, mix the ingredients for the seasoning.

(3) Coat both sides of the tofu in the seasoning mixture.

(4) In a frying pan, heat 1 Tbs of vegetable oil and 2 Tbs of butter. Slowly sauté the tofu on all sides until the pieces are nicely browned. Set it aside on warmed serving plates.

(5) In the same pan, add the remaining vegetable oil and butter. Add the mushrooms and sauté. When mushrooms are cooked, add all the sauce ingredients except the fresh cream and cook for 1 minute. Let the mixture blend well with the mushroom. Add the fresh cream at the end and remove from heat.

(6) Pour the mushroom sauce over the tofu and serve.

Keiko's Original Healthy Lean Tofu Hamburger

(Serves 4)

Cooking Time 20 minutes

Hamburgers may be all-American, but Americans are gaining too much weight from eating fat-laden beef patties. When I feel like having a hearty but healthy meal, I make tofu hamburgers. This dish allows you to provide your family with the protein they need in a healthy manner.

Ingredients:

silken tofu	1 cake
ground chicken	7 oz
onion—finely chopped	½ medium-sized
cherry tomatoes	7 oz
broccoli	½ bunch
vegetable oil	1 Tbs
butter	1 Tbs
Worcestershire sauce	1 Tbs
salt	to taste

Seasoning:

panko	½ cup
egg—lightly beaten	1
salt	1 tsp
sugar	½ tsp
nutmeg	to taste
pepper	to taste

Directions:

(1)   Wrap the tofu in a paper towel and place it on a plate. Microwave for 1 minute at high to remove excess moisture.

(2)   Cut the cherry tomatoes in half. In small frying pan sauté the cherry tomatoes in 1 Tbs butter. Once the cherry tomatoes are tender, add 1 Tbs of Worcestershire sauce. Remove from heat and set aside.

(3)   In a small pan, heat ½ Tbs of vegetable oil and sauté the onion. Set aside to cool.

(4)   Boil the broccoli in salted water. Drain and set aside.

(5)   In a small bowl, place the ground chicken, onion, and the seasoning ingredients. Break the tofu into small pieces and mix well with all the ingredients. Shape the mixture into 4 small hamburgers.

(6)   To fry the patties, heat ½ Tbs of vegetable oil on medium heat and cook them for 2 minutes. Turn the patties over and set the heat to low. Cook for 6 to 8 minutes until inside is done.

(7)   Place hamburgers on a plate. Serve with the tomatoes and broccoli.

Agedashi Tofu

(Serves 4)

Cooking Time: 20 minutes

I am bit of a health freak and I like to eat a lot of tofu. My American friends love this dish when I make it for them. They always think it's hard, but I taught them the way I make it which is quite easy and simple.

Ingredients:

firm tofu	2 cakes
onion—finely minced	3 Tbs
caviar	for garnish
potato starch (katakuriko)	¼ cup
vegetable oil	for frying
Japanese dried seaweed—cut in stips	for garnish

Sauce:

dashi stock	1 cup
soy sauce	3 Tbs
mirin	3 Tbs

Directions:

(1) Wrap the tofu cakes in a paper towel and place them on a plate. Microwave for 1 minute at high to remove excess moisture.

(2) Put the sauce ingredients in a small pot and bring to a boil. Remove from heat and set aside.

(3) On a plate, coat all sides of tofu with the Japanese potato starch.

(4) Heat the vegetable oil in a pan to 340°. Fry the tofu until it is lightly browned.

(5) Place the tofu in a small bowl and pour the sauce over it. Garnish with minced onion, caviar, and seaweed.

Desserts

甘味

Heavenly Ginger Vanilla

(Serves 4)

Cooking Time: 5 minutes

This unexpected combination of flavors makes a great way to end a meal.

Ingredients:

vanilla ice cream	2 scoops

Sauce:

mirin	½ cup
ginger—grated	1 1-inch knob

Directions:

(1)   Pour mirin in a pan and bring to a boil. Add the ginger, remove from heat and let it cool.

(2)   Serve the vanilla ice cream in a bowl and pour the sauce over the top. It's that easy!

Sweet & Dreamy Baked Potato

(Serves 4)

Cooking Time: 20 minutes

This dessert not only tastes great, but you also get the healthy nutrients of the sweet potato.

Ingredients:

sweet potato	1 medium-sized
egg yolk—lightly beaten	1

Seasoning:

butter	1 Tbs
brown sugar	3 Tbs
fresh cream	2 Tbs

Directions:

(1) In a bowl, mix seasoning ingredients and set aside.

(2) Peel the sweet potato and cut into 8 to 10 pieces. Wet a paper towel and wrap the sweet potato with it. Place on a microwave-safe plate and cover with clear plastic wrap. Microwave for 8 minutes on high.

(3) When the potato is cooked, mash it and mix in the seasoning.

(4) Make the potato mix into circular shaped patties 1-inch thick. Using a pastry brush, brush the egg yolk on top.

(5) Place the patties on a baking sheet and bake in toaster oven for 8 minutes.

Index